Your Home, Your Castle

A Boomer's Guide— How to Prepare for Homecare

CHUCK OAKES

Copyright © 2014 Chuck Oakes
All rights reserved.

ISBN: 1495211800
ISBN 13: 9781495211805

Preface

If you are just starting your care-giving role, you are about to embark on a rewarding but often exhausting journey. This text is written for you...to learn from my personal experiences with the intent to make your journey safer and more effective... and perhaps more enjoyable.

You're reading this text or perhaps listening to it while on your treadmill. Perhaps because some kind soul gave it to you for the holidays, or your birthday, or maybe you bought it yourself due to an urgent family need. In any case, the idea of caring for an elderly parent, or perhaps caring for a child with disabilities can be daunting. Having been a caregiver for my parents for several years, I am <u>intimately familiar</u> with the *chores and challenges* (and surprises) associated with the role. You have time to read this text because, frankly, you haven't hit bottom yet!! When you're deep in the trenches, you don't have time for much other than essentials. Don't misunderstand me; I would not trade my experience caring for my parents for anything! It was indeed a gift to be able to support and serve THEM, as they did their family, for so many years.

My first text on aging, **MAKING YOUR HOME SENIOR-FRIENDLY,** was written in preparation for homecare and support of aging loved ones, in their own homes…or perhaps your home. This sequel take a slightly more energized look at the situation, that is, we now take a more urgent look at the subject of homecare. Most families wait to renovate or enhance their homes for eldercare until a "life incident", such as a broken hip. So, we begin this journey with the "phone call" from Boca Raton when your Mom's doctor says that she fell and broke her hip in Florida and will be returning to live with you after rehab!! Yes, it is indeed, time to smell the java and "ramp it up a bit"!

Although the majority of caregivers are women, sons often step up to the plate and help out, whether by choice or circumstance…(or sibling pressure). As a guy, I wanted to step-it-up a bit and add some testosterone to the text, both visually and in overall approach.

Everyone's home is <u>*their castle*</u>…make it as enjoyable as you can.

Gillette Castle State Park, Hadlyme, CT on the Connecticut River

*M**any of the shots included in this text were taken at this state park. It has become one of my favorite places. I became associated with the park as its first* **President of the Friends of Gillette Castle State Park** *for several years. For years, I felt a special connection with William Gillette. We had much in common; both in our careers and our personal passions. (Rustic furniture and trains, for instance). Being* <u>his retirement home</u> *during the turn of the last century, it is fitting that it be our visual backdrop for this book—his home was, in point of fact—his castle!*

Table of Contents

Preface iii

Gillette Castle State Park, Hadlyme, CT on the
Connecticut River v

About the Inspiration ix

Chapter 1   Preparing for the Journey 1

Chapter 2   Safety & Security Matters 5

Chapter 3   *Creative Cuisine* for Caregivers 11

Chapter 4   Hiring the Homecare Team 19

Chapter 5   Collecting the Data 25

Chapter 6   Making Your Home *Sensory-Supported* 35

Chapter 7   "The Game Changer—Mom's Broken Hip . . . 47

Chapter 8   Painful Lessons Learned.................. 53

Chapter 9   Legacy Matters.......................... 57

Chapter 10   Helpful Information and Resources........ 65

About the Author.................................... 73

Testimonial.. 75

About the Inspiration

This book is dedicated in loving memory of my parents, who were my inspiration and examples of *"Graceful Aging"*.

Marie L. Oakes
1919-2009

Arthur C. Oakes
1918-2006

CHAPTER ONE

Preparing for the Journey

Most of us usually wait until an emergency to do something; that is, we wait to close the barn door after the horse is stolen. The other day, I received a frantic call from a friend whose husband had just suffered a heart attack and was in the hospital. In tears, she asked for my help in getting him home where she could care for him with dignity.

After consoling her on the phone, I asked her a few basic questions:

1. What is his prognosis? How extensive or severe is his condition?
2. When can he be released and under what conditions?
3. What financial resources are available to the family? How many family members or friends are available to take care of him? How much time do the caregivers have available to help out?
4. What will be his needs at home? Will he require special devices, support and medical care to reside at home?

Addressing these basic questions enabled us to determine the feasibility of getting him home safely and securely while providing the appropriate support.

When providing homecare, it is essential to take a look at the whole picture; that is, what is best for everyone…including the needs of the caregiver. In setting up priorities, it is essential that one take into account the limitations of available resources. For instance, when I hired Certified Nursing Assistants to help both Mom and Dad, I scheduled them for no longer than 6-hour shifts at any one time. I was always asked why I did that. My response was that I had no intention of replacing staff every three months, as is the average, so I was told. As a human resource professional, I understand the benefits of supporting the caregiving team. Keeping the work shift hours down to a manageable 6 hours prevents burnout, stress and irritability.

Recalling my days as a caregiver, I remember the constant uncertainty and related pressures of the job and how after 100-hour workweeks, I was becoming irritable and resentful for the responsibilities and the "life sacrifices" I was experiencing because of my role. When I say "sacrifices" I mean that dedicated caregivers, whether family members or others, make enormous sacrifices to those they support in terms of the time and life experiences they often miss because of their commitment to their care-receiver.

A state legislator told me the other day that all too often caregivers die before those they care for do! Someone else told me that about 20% of caregivers die prematurely; while this figure is unsubstantiated, the amount is too high!

A prescription for healthy care giving (from someone who has been there):

- Know your limitations…physical, mental, emotional, availability, etc.
- Practice healthy personal habits…nutrition, rest, exercise, etc.
- Integrate some "fun" into your life to maintain healthy energy and enthusiasm…which carries over into your work. This could include hobbies, crafts, sports, family time, reading, etc. Too often, our society equates having fun with "goofing off". Who says we have to be serious and productive at all times? Actually, studies have shown the benefits of endorphins created by physical exercise and laughter! It's true that laughing can have health benefits.

- Stay connected. Be a part or member of something. Join and become connected to a larger association or organization. For example, this could be a religious affiliation or club. But it is important to feel a part of something larger…to be valued and appreciated also helps.
- Go easy on yourself. We are often too tough on ourselves and have unrealistic expectations for those around us…and ourselves. Not only does this practice make us boring to be with, but lack of enjoyment can have serious consequences to our wellness in terms of our immune systems.
- When possible, be with positive, uplifting people. It really helps when you are inspired by and surrounded by energized people.
- We all need to be recognized and (hopefully) appreciated for our efforts. The lack of such compensation can have a long-term affect on our self-image and wellness. The care giving role is thankless and the "return-on-investment" is often inadequate, especially compared with traditional day jobs. Hence, we must realize WHY we are in this role and align our expectations accordingly. If we are looking for *recognition and reward*, get another job or seek these in other aspects of your life (hobbies, clubs, volunteering, sports, crafts, etc.)
- As time allows, learn something…perhaps a musical instrument, a language, computer skill, craft or hobby.

"Balance and blend" is the best practice for maintaining wellness and health, especially in jobs that are stressful and thankless.

CHAPTER TWO

Safety & Security Matters

In preparation for your aging loved one returning home, or perhaps moving in with you, the residence must be *safe and*

secure in order to become *"senior-friendly"*. That is, you should evaluate the home as you would child-proofing it...but at an elevated level. The extent and scope of renovations depends on the needs and abilities of the residents and whether they live alone or not.

Special care is required for special needs. For example, residents with dementia/Alzheimer's Disease require greater attention in a variety of ways, including daily support and security (in the event of wandering, getting lost, etc.). This text will cover the basics for the general aging population. If your family is facing "special needs", I suggest you continue your research regarding appropriate services and supportive resources.

Basic considerations include the following:

- **Faucets in kitchens** can have gooseneck design for ease of use, especially for individuals suffering with arthritis.
- **Bathrooms should have support bars** in tubs and perhaps walk-in tubs. Be sure there are no rugs in the room.
- **Adjustable kitchen cupboards** can be modified to accommodate the residents...and laundry machines can be elevated for easier access.
- **Closet lighting** throughout the house should be adequate and preferably motion-activated, or automatic.
- **Hot water temperature** should not be too hot. It is recommended to use 140 degrees F as the preferred maximum setting.
- **As we mentioned in bathrooms, throw away the throw rugs throughout the home. They** are hazards and can cause trips and slips. If you *must* keep them, make sure they have adhesive backing to prevent slips and slides.

- **Door handles** can be replaced by levers, which are easier to "*handle*". (pun intended)
- **Keyless entry systems** are easier to use than those with keys. Some of them even turn on your house lights from a key fob!
- **Motion-detector lights** can prevent falls and burglaries. These can be used inside or outside…in entryways, basements, garages, etc.

Security for Seniors

While caregivers focus on "safety matters" for aging loved ones, it is also critical to prepare for <u>security matters</u>. People with disabilities, including the elderly are especially vulnerable to scams and criminal intent. Here are some pointers to prevent home invasion:

- **Signs** such as "Beware of Dog" and "Security System Used Here" can reduce crime and deter unwanted intruders. There are plenty of unprotected homes in every community, so by taking some inexpensive, logical deterrents, you can reduce your chance of becoming a victim.
- **Emergency Alert devices, such as First Alert** can provide peace of mind by helping summon emergency personnel in times of distress and breaches of security. They were originally designed to summon help for <u>medical issues</u> through the use of bracelets or neck pendants, but can also be used in the event that someone comes to the door who looks suspicious. By pressing the button on the device, the service can actually monitor the conversation and determine if there is a potential problem…and act accordingly.

Beware of Unsolicited Solicitors!

Many communities regulate and license door-to-door salespersons but NOT those who are recruiting, assessing antiques, or come to the door for other *non-sales* reasons. It is this writer's judgment that solicitation is all the same and should all be regulated to protect all residents...of all ages. Therefore, beware of the danger of allowing strangers into your community or your house. Never let anyone into the house without credentials. Many communities regulate who solicits business from door to door, but not always antique appraisals, religious organizations, etc. **ANYONE approaching your door should have credentials readily available,** or activate First Alert button, which will summon help. Call local police when uncertain of the guest at the door. **Install peepholes** in doors when possible.

- "Curb Appearance"—Entryway ramps into the house can send a message of "vulnerability" to criminals. Such ramps should be visually minimized and out of sight when feasible.

Information on Contractors

The **National Association of Home Builders**, in conjunction with AARP, developed a certification program called, **CERTIFIED AGING IN PLACE SPECIALIST, CAPS**. The author has been certified. Why is this important, you ask? When a contractor is CAPS certified, you can be certain that they have been properly trained as to the legal and safe methods of home improvements for seniors. The program covers industry standards with seniors in mind.

Contractors for home renovations and other work should always provide credentials, estimates and references before doing any work on your premises. They should also provide evidence of insurance should something go wrong on the job. Work with established vendors. Check with local resources, such as the Chamber of Commerce or Better Business Bureau before committing to any contractor.

Common Sense Goes a Long Way

Residents living alone should have visitors or people calling them daily...by phone or in person.

Suggestions

Sense of smell is critical, especially when detecting spoiled foods. It is helpful to have dates on all foods in the refrigerator and check them for spoilage.

Keep Information Inside of Refrigerator Door

Many towns' Social Services Departments provide a magnetized label to be attached to the refrigerator door. The accompanying vial, located inside the door, should contain helpful information, such as doctors' contact information, key family members (and their caregiving roles) and **Do Not Resuscitate** (DNR) papers in addition to other pertinent information such as allergies, etc. It is critical that such important information be readily available for emergency personnel.

CHAPTER THREE

Creative Cuisine for Caregivers

In most of the discussions about caregiving and supporting our seniors, we focus on "bricks and mortar", procedures, finances, legalities, policies and finances. Somewhere in the mix, we often forget about the *joy and happiness* of life. Mealtime is a perfect example of an important, daily routine that normally brings family members together, even though that practice has eroded in recent decades. But seniors remember family gatherings around the dinner table and enjoying special times with those they love. Mealtimes become even more important towards the end of life, because they are daily social events.

In senior years, things change and we find our loved ones in retirement communities, healthcare facilities or alone at home. Hardly the joyous and happy times of yesteryear.

In Our Home

There are numerous factors that effect the enjoyment of mealtimes and getting sufficient nutrition. These factors include:

- Lack of appetite
- Lack of exercise
- Medication influence on diet, taste, appetite
- Potential aspiration/choking (swallowing difficulties)
- Allergies
- Dehydration
- Constipation
- Urinary tract infections (UTI)
- Diverticulitus (and related conditions)

Our bodies require *fewer calories* due to a reduced need for calories and the effects of certain medications. One of the recurring challenges for us was the need for adequate hydration. My folks were reluctant to drink sufficient fluids because of the consequences of frequent visits to the bathroom. So, we found that Urinary Tract Infections (UTI) were all too common. The frequency of these episodes necessitated medication on a regular basis.

So the challenge for caregivers is to maintain (or regain) the enjoyment of mealtimes while getting your folks to eat enough.

My brother and I were raised to become self-sufficient in life and domestic chores. In our home, the kitchen became a site for personal expression and creativity. Mom urged us to use recipes as "starting suggestions" but to use our imaginations and creativity to explore new meals.

Nutrition

By now, you are undoubtedly aware of the various kinds of nutritional supplements and how they add calories and nutrition, mostly in liquid form. One of the Aides called me one day and said that Mom was not drinking enough. I asked, "What are you giving her?" She said, a nutritional supplement." Straight, no chaser, no mixer…nothing! I asked the Aide, "Would *you* drink it *straight*?" To which she replied, "No way!" "So why on earth would you expect her to drink it that way?" (Time to think "out of the box"!) We had a blender and we got some ice cream, or sherbet/sorbet, and went wild! For example, Mom always enjoyed adding mint to her brownies…the blend of mint and chocolate was really refreshing, so, we added some chocolate mint ice cream to her chocolate supplement, creating a tasty, nutritional culinary experience that *actually worked*!! I asked the Aides *not* to make a big deal out of it, but simply to mix up the concoction around 2 or 3pm and give her a small glass of it... without making it an ordeal or obligation. "Just slip it in front of her, stand back, and watch what happens." *She loved it!*

Aging Taste Buds

As for the *flavors themselves*, remember that **taste buds are aging** and therefore, seniors are more apt to recognize *spicy and sweet* tastes. Perhaps you have experienced seniors enjoying their sweets more than earlier in life. It might be that it has something to do with aging taste buds and the "sweet tooth" as one of the remaining "active" senses. For example, if you're using vanilla in milkshakes, try adding extra vanilla to the vanilla ice cream or flavored supplement. Vanilla is mild and might not get on their "radar". You might need to *boost* it up a bit with added extract. Chocolate is generally more powerful and does not require much enhancement, in my experience.

Meal Frequency

After several discussions, our team came up with a routine of *nutritional exploration*, which consisted of **grazing** at several times during the day with a lighter meal portion in the evening. For those unfamiliar with the idea, I refer to grazing as simply a series of smaller meals and portions 4-5 times during the day, rather than three larger meals, which many of us are traditionally accustomed to.

In addition to the smaller, more frequent culinary "bites" through the day, we established the routine of a mid-morning "smoothie break". From our California influence early in my childhood, I learned to appreciate mangos, papayas and guavas. And since several of our Aides were Jamaican, we loved many of the same foods and condiments, including ginger, hot peppers and tropical fruits. As you can imagine, our fruit smoothies became a tropical explosion of flavors that my folks could actually taste and enjoy. The mid-morning break, around 10am, became the smoothie break.

Try Variety—*Mix It Up!*

As for traditional entrees, I remember Mom saying that *"I'm so sick of chicken, even if they're giving them away ...don't buy them!"* Therefore, we prepared fish, turkey, meatloaf and shellfish frequently...with an occasional chicken thrown into the mix when Mom wasn't looking. The next challenge was: How do we get them to actually eat and hopefully enjoy our preparations? Well, we relied on no-salt, no MSG flavor enhancements. When preparing poultry and tuna, remember the aging taste buds. We needed to *kick it up a notch* to get the meal on the radar! So out came the red pepper (also good for the heart), garlic, rosemary, savory, oregano and marjoram. My folks especially liked my preparation of salmon....using ginger, sesame and teriyaki to enhance the dish. I often drizzled maple syrup over fish before serving it, fresh from the oven or skillet. We did not fry anything.

Swallowing Matters—*it truly does!*

Another point to keep in mind is that many seniors have **digestive** challenges **and swallowing problems.** Beware of dishes with seeds, nuts, corn and other foods that can cause problems. Specifically, diverticulitis, (colon problem) can be exacerbated by eating seeds, which can get caught in the intestines and tear the lining...not a good thing (especially when one is on blood thinners! Mom almost died when taking a blood thinner with her diverticulitis.) Dad had swallowing issues, (aspiration) and therefore, we had to be advised how best to help him swallow safely without relying on food-thickeners, (often prescribed to avoid aspirating...which is when food goes into the lungs due to issues in the throat.) Thankfully, we did not rely on the thickener. Using the thickener, which is a white powder when added to liquids, makes them thick and easier to safely swallow and thus not get improperly *directed* into the lungs. For those caregivers who have used thickeners, they do not *add* to the mealtime experience; but they must be considered when aspiration is a potential.

Mealtimes Have Changed

Mealtimes have been traditionally a time when families gather to share their experiences of the day and enjoy a meal together. Times have changed and for too many families meals no longer include all family members. For most seniors, not only are they not with their families but also their enjoyment of mealtimes has changed. In fact, many retirement communities are now revamping the manner in which they prepare and serve meals...in order to bring back the civility and enjoyment of mealtime for seniors. At a recent meeting, I was informed that a community was instructed NOT to stand over seniors while they eat from their trays....but rather, many have been instructed NOT to use trays at all and to sit with the residents rather than hovering over them! These are steps in the right direction...prompted by the **Pioneer Network, Planetree** and other similar advocates for change in healthcare and eldercare.

Scents Make Sense! *(But be mindful of allergies)*

Studies have shown that certain aromas can stimulate the appetite. Consider using vanilla, cinnamon and apple to enhance the environment, especially around the kitchen or before meals. Think of it; who doesn't love the smell of freshly baked cookies, brownies...anytime of the day? Try flameless candles or even room sprays. To illustrate my point, Muzak, the reigning kind of sound enhancements for restaurants, hotels, malls and other public places, now offers specific aromas that can be used to further enhance their music options...all designed to improve and enhance the impact and effect of our surroundings by creating the desired results using our senses.

Summary of Suggestions:

- Serve smaller portions
- Grazing and frequent snacks throughout the day
- Primary meal at noontime

- Flavor enhancements (preferably without salt and MSG or otherwise prescribed by nurse, nutritionist or doctor)
- Thickener when needed to prevent aspiration
- Use food processor to make it easier to eat and digest food
- Consider soothing background music to relax and foster pleasant eating experiences. (Some retirement homes provide live music at mealtimes.)
- Smoothies and "enhanced shakes" to aid hydration
- Aromas might help enhance mealtime enjoyment before, during or after the meal

CHAPTER FOUR

Hiring the Homecare Team

At some point in your journey, you might need to consider recruiting some help to provide the homecare your family needs. Perhaps you've done all you can and the needs, medical or domestic, surpass your capabilities. Whether you live close by or far away, eldercare must be respectful, consistent and effective.

It is always best to introduce the idea of homecare *before* it is required. As it became evident that my parents preferred to remain at home, we discussed their needs, desires and finances. We developed a plan of action that would enable them to remain at home for as long as feasible. Now, the healthcare industry refers to this as *"aging-in-place"*.

We began our journey into homecare/eldercare with a **needs assessment.** The doctor and our family discussed the present and anticipated conditions of Mom and Dad and proceeded to design home modifications that acknowledged personal preferences, abilities, dignity and safety. Many towns have Case Managers who are qualified to evaluate the needs of your parents.

Considering that my only sibling was three hours away while I was a mere 20 minutes, I became the primary caregiver for our parents. It was up to me to manage the care and support for them.

I started with daily visits and then chose specific times when I could be useful in doing a variety of chores, as it became evident that their abilities were soon dictating need for enhanced care on a regular basis. Initially, I found myself devoting more than 100 hours per week in direct and indirect care for them! Well, it didn't take long before I was destined for disaster! I was crashing and about to burn. About this time, Mom broke her hip, which escalated matters considerably.

While Mom was in the hospital and subsequent rehabilitation, I took advantage of the opportunity to have modifications done to the home, in preparation for her return. These modifications included replacing door knobs with levers, adding a gooseneck fixture in the kitchen sink to facilitate washing her hair, railings and other enhancements to help with transitions between rooms, etc. (Details are outlined in Chapter Two.)

Where to Find Qualified Assistance

When you have discovered that you need reinforcements to provide more care than the family can provide, there are several places to look, depending upon your resources and finances.

- Religious associations/churches/temples, etc.
- Town hall
- Local senior centers
- Nursing and healthcare schools/colleges

- Employment agencies that specialize in healthcare
- Neighbors, friends and family members

Domestic and Medical Needs

Once you get an updated "status report" from your Case Manager (from the town or healthcare agency) and/or your family physician, you can proceed to secure help. With this information, you will be better informed as to what you need to seek out in assistance.

Levels of Care

There are essentially **three levels** of professional care, which pertain to supporting seniors:

- **Companion/homemaker**—these individuals provide non-medical, domestic help, such as cooking, cleaning and companionship...perhaps even driving to appointments, etc. Be aware that this level of service has limitations. For instance, when Mom was in rehab for her hip surgery, I hired a companion to supplement hospital/rehab staff on the overnight shift...just to be safe. I was later informed that the level of certification/training of a *companion* _prohibited them_ from actually TOUCHING Mom in an effort to prevent a fall or injury! A higher level of care was required to actually prevent injury.
- **Certified Nursing Assistants**—these professionals are trained to administer basic healthcare/medical services

and give out medication. While they can give out medication, they cannot fill the pillboxes (for legal reasons, this must be done by nurses).
- **Registered Nurses**—provide expert medical and health-care-related services. Normally they manage homecare providers through an agency or in a facility. Be aware that if you hire homecare workers directly and NOT through an agency, visiting nurses cannot direct or give instructions to your homecare aide. My family solved this dilemma by having the visiting nurses write down their comments, observations and directives onto a sheet of paper…to be read by homecare workers at a later time. Since the nurse does NOT work for or with the aides you hired, the nurse cannot (legally) communicate directly to them. Nurses are responsible for filling the weekly pillboxes, when used.

In summary, you must carefully evaluate and match the proper care for your loved ones with the appropriate care provider. In addition to certification and training, some other considerations include:

- Language proficiency
- Ability to cook
- Do they have a license to drive? There might be times when driving is important…such as, driving to doctors' appointments.
- Are they willing to buy groceries?
- Do they play games or do craftwork?
- Do they have a special talent to share? (musical instrument, hobby, etc.)

Sample interview and introduction forms are included for your consideration.

Once hired, your team needs to be introduced to your parents. I did this with a detailed written overview, or "Profile" of my parents. Such an introduction provided all the information a caregiver needed to do their job as quickly and seamlessly as possible; the written profile reduced confusion or doubt about their care needs and wishes. As for actual job expectations and requirements, I prepared a **Job Description** with all the details for the specific job for which they were being hired, including hours of work, compensation, etc.

Employee Relations—Performance Recognition...*Plus More*

Like every worker, caregivers need to be recognized for excellence and superior performance. I had *"Certificates of Excellence"* printed for outstanding performance. Birthdays were celebrated. In addition to holiday gifts, I gave them each a severance payment upon the termination of their employment (at the death of my parents). Even after the death of my parents, I hosted *Team Reunions* every two months to celebrate life, love and health...while remembering my parents and all that the team did to make their lives safe and enjoyable at home. At these reunions, I usually cooked the entrée and they provided side dishes. It was always a welcome and festive occasion to get together as a "family". As with all families, we experienced some challenges and sadness...one aide suffered a stroke, another had cancer ...and another was looking for work. No one is immune from the *sting of reality!* It is in these difficult times that the true character of friendship becomes clear.

It has also become clear that the wealth of a person is not in the goods they possess, or the items they bequeath, but in the lives they've touched in their life journey.

When hiring homecare assistants, it is essential that you protect yourself and your family with the proper documentation and procedures. While your Department of Labor or Senior Services might be of help, there are some key elements that must be included in all employment contracts:

- Complete names and aliases, former names, etc.
- All addresses for the past 6 years
- At least three (non-related) references
- The employment agreement (might be) "employment at will"; employees can be terminated without cause. This is not always the case, hence, check with your state DOL.
- In your agreement letter, indicate that your family reserves the right to use video surveillance systems and equipment on the premises.

Reference Checking is mandatory and can be done through your local Police Services department or Homecare agency.

CHAPTER FIVE

Collecting the Data

As you might have experienced, there are essentially three phases of **aging-at-home**:

1. Preparation for homecare
2. "In the trenches"…delivery of care
3. Preparing for the final days.

Preparing for homecare is never easy or comfortable, especially for family members. As with other sections of this text, this chapter is a summary of some of my experiences and suggestions in data collection for your present and future as primary caregiver. Such advance preparation will make your journey more sensitive, secure and comfortable. Consultation with professionals is advised, especially in areas pertaining to legal and financial matters.

Just the other day, my brother said to me, "If you die, we're in deep trouble!" *(Aside from my personal desires for care and comfort at the end of my life, as primary caregiver for our parents, I was the "point person" for details of their care, including location of bank accounts, etc.)*

Here are some salient points to consider as you continue your caregiving and ultimately, prepare for the end-of-life ….yours and those you support.

Documentation

To make this easy, I have separated the information and documentation into two categories…the *short list* and the *enhanced version*. **The short list** is for immediate, critical contacts and documents that your family will need to know about and be able to locate for making decisions about care. The **enhanced**

version is simply an extended listing of affiliations and contacts. To maintain your sanity and calm during the process of preparing these items, I suggest you tackle "small doses" at a time; otherwise, it is easy to become overwhelmed.

By now you undoubtedly have found out that the most important basic facts you must have available as the caregiver are your <u>parent(s) social security numbers and birth dates</u>. Unfortunately, this information is too often used for identification and security purposes. If you haven't experienced it yet, you will be asked to provide a <u>legal release</u> in writing...giving permission (to an organization, bank, etc.) to share confidential, privileged and private information about your parents. After their death, you will need to provide death certificates to many institutions that your parents dealt with.

The Short List

This abbreviated listing should be accessible near every phone in the house to be used in times of emergencies. The list can also be used for long-term planning.

In the event of emergencies, the list should include:

- Address of your location
- Pharmacy contact information
- Primary care physician
- Religious affiliation/contact person
- Contacts of family members and closest friends

The following documents should be available in the home, but not necessary at bedside. We have mentioned that many towns provide a vial or canister for such information to be kept in the refrigerator with a magnet on the door to alert emergency personnel of its location.

- List of all medications
- Legal documents (Power of Attorney, Healthcare Agent, Trustees/Executors, DNR, etc.) (These documents should be *available* at the house when needed.)

The Longer List

- Advisors
    - Bankers
    - Insurance agent
    - Investment professionals, financial planners and stock brokers
    - Attorney
    - Accountant
    - Veterinarian (yes, pets matter also)

- Documents related to the following:
    - Stock certificates
    - Adoption
    - Annuities
    - Annulments and divorce documents
    - Marriage licenses
    - Mortgages
    - Death certificates
    - Deeds
    - Guardianship

- Wills
- Advance directives/preferences (healthcare and organ donations, etc.)
- Partnership agreements
- Prenuptial agreements
- Letters or recordings (audio/video) to be mailed upon death
- Pension plans
- Birth certificates
- Titles to car, boat, etc.
- Cemetery deeds
- Credit cards
- Magazine subscriptions to cancel
- Memberships to notify and cancel upon death
    - Religious affiliations
    - Professional associations
    - Clubs
    - Charities
    - Veterans groups
    - Fraternal organizations
- Bank accounts
    - Be aware that after death, bank accounts must be changed, unless they are joint accounts.

Hospice Care

When the physician has determined that the end of life is near, usually less than six months away, a comprehensive support "package" is available. The services include medical, case management (the overall supervision of care) and domestic support (non-medical services that enable the patient to remain at home). It is my experience that hospice care is paid for by Medicare/Medicaid or insurance, but check with your insurance carrier first. It is important to note that hospice will provide support, respite and related services for family members. In some cases, Hospice care can make "death at home" more civilized and easier on the family because they can interact with emergency personnel and police services, as needed. Death at home procedures and complications vary depending upon specific town regulations.

When Mom grew weaker, we considered implementing hospice care, but our team and household were set up already for this level of support.

Advance Directives/Preparation for Final Days

Medical Directives—Living Will

Specific preferences must be defined and in writing. These include:

"Do Not Resuscitate" (DNR), is a legal document that clearly outlines the extent to which resuscitation or other life support can be used for your loved one. We are all familiar with the bracelets that indicate DNR preference, but sometimes these bracelets fall off. Hence, to be safe and sure, make all relevant documentation available at the home for visiting medical personnel. Do not rely on the bracelet (DNR) alone.

Organ Donors

On drivers' licenses, there is a designation of whether the driver is an organ donor. If not a driver, this preference can be included in advance directives.

Healthcare Agent

This is a legal form, which identifies the person who is responsible for managing the care for your loved one; it could be a family member or someone else. As Dad was in his last moments, the doctor and I discussed and administered the proper dose of pain medication. The healthcare agent works closely with medical staff to ensure compliance with the wishes of the family and patient.

Financial & Legal Matters—Trustee and Executor

These legal designations are essential for the management of the family's finances, during and after life.

Durable Power of Attorney

When guiding your family through the journey of homecare/eldercare, someone must take charge. Usually, the family physician makes the determination that the patient is no longer capable of managing his or her own affairs, and this written statement is then provided to an elder law attorney (preferred, but not essential...elder law), who completes the form for Power of Attorney. This designation terminates at the time of the patient's death.

Examples of the importance of prior planning and preparation—

- o We have discussed the need for a collection point for a listing of all medications and some legal documentation. The refrigerator door is where emergency personnel are accustomed to look for them. As I suggested, I strongly advise that you also include a summary of designations/family responsibilities such as DNR, Power of Attorney and Healthcare Agent paperwork. Be aware that under certain circumstances, family members (or legal representatives) may have to provide supportive documentation upon request.

Beyond the legal and financial preparations associated with end of life, there are some sensitive and caring considerations you should think about.

Every time I saw Mom, I thought that this might be the last moment with her...and I treated her accordingly. This is not morbid, but a sober reality that in her condition, every day is a blessing and should be cherished with appropriate respect and reverence.

Ideas to consider in preparing for *the final days:*

1. Technology today can be very useful in capturing family memories. Audio and video recordings can help preserve sensory elements of the family and times together.

Not only do these recordings serve as documentation for archival purposes, they can be fun to look back on in the future.
2. Social networks can provide an efficient way to communicate to your friends and family members. Consider Facebook, LinkedIn and other vehicles. For privacy and security reasons, be careful about including too many details. (Burglaries often occur while families are attending funerals.)
3. Have your parents write their own "Life Story." This comes in handy when writing obituaries. When you, or an Aide, transcribes this, you might consider recording it…to add another dimension to the process.
4. Master Mailing List—friends and family members
    a. Prepare a master mailing/email list of family members and friends to contact but while your parents are alive. Such a list can come in handy after they are gone. Sometimes out-of-town people never are notified of deaths. Out of sight…out of mind is too often the case in aging. When people move out of town, they are often not included in correspondence or communication. I have referred to this list to keep in touch around the holidays with people who were close to my family.

Funeral and Burial Basics:

(The master listing mentioned earlier can provide many details.)
Here are some items to consider when preparing for the funeral service and/or burial:

- Cremation or burial?
- Preferred notification list (designated friends and affiliations to be notified at death)
- Notification for specific associations, affiliations, clubs, etc.
- Monument type (if any)
- Epitaph (as appropriate)
- Preferred funeral home
- Obituary (it really helps to have this prepared in advance. Having loved ones write a "Life Story" is one way to prepare.)
- Memorial service _____(where) by ___(pastor, clergy, etc.)
  - Music _____(specifics) to be performed by ____(artist)
  - Favorite hymns or bible/scripture verses _____
  - Closed ___or open casket
  - Recording of service (by professional, family member....or not at all)
  - Philanthropic affiliations (Were arrangements made for donations to charities upon death?)
  - Friends, family members to speak during service
  - Collect favorite pictures for poster, bulletins, etc.
  - Multi-media presentation given during service.... with or without background music
- Prepaid funeral expenses? It is always best to secure funeral arrangements BEFORE you need them! Pay for them in advance, so your family does not have to be burdened by them when you are gone.

CHAPTER SIX

Making Your Home *Sensory-Supported*

Quality of life is greatly influenced by the manner in which we relate and respond to our surroundings...through our *senses*. Hence, as we enhance our homes for our aging loved ones, and ourselves, we should utilize *all* the sensory elements possible.

Our ability to interact with our surroundings changes as our sensory abilities decline...as we age. So, the challenge becomes how to maximize the benefits of those "active" senses we still enjoy.

In my earlier text, **MAKING YOUR HOME SENIOR-FRIENDLY**, you will find an introduction to sensory support. In this text, we will continue this creative approach to home preparation for aging.

Lighting

As our visual acuity diminishes with age, we must pay particular attention to lighting our environment for both existing and anticipated challenges. Lighting should be supportive and functional. For instance, if you are using lighting to prevent injuries, trips, falls and accidents, it should be definitive and strong. Workstations, such as the kitchen, should have powerful and clear lighting.

Example

In the bedroom, Mom used a commode, which was about 7 feet from her bed. Mom fell once while accessing the commode and Dad tripped over it while walking past it. It is from accidents that we learn...the hard way! Changes had to be made to correct risks of injury. The first thing we addressed was to secure the commode to the wall. This prevented the commode from moving and tipping.

Bedroom Lighting

Mom and Dad slept in the same room in separate beds. Dad was the "keeper of the light" all night; when Mom needed to get up, he was responsible for activating the room light, enabling Mom to get to and from the commode safely. As anticipated, this arrangement lasted a month or so, before it wore him out... needlessly. So, I installed an inexpensive lighting system that relieved Dad from his responsibility and allowed him to sleep better. This system was comprised of a button-activated extension cord--the kind often used to activate holiday lighting--and a string of lights, (small ones, often used during the holidays). With this system, Mom was able to activate and *manage her own lighting* when she needed to get up in the middle of the night, without disrupting Dad.

It is worth noting that as Mom's eyesight diminished further, the string of holiday lights were replaced with a direct light (aimed at the commode). This light was activated by a motion-detector, which required no manual action from Mom. Soon thereafter, Dad passed away unexpectedly and an Aide provided more support for Mom at night.

Indirect lighting—Soft, Supportive and Soothing

For individuals with failing eyesight, shadows can be problematic. Therefore, indirect lighting is best for most applications throughout the house, with exception for work areas or to highlight specific dangers (steps, commodes, walkways, etc.) I used *soft pastel lighting* under Mom's bed to bathe the floor with supportive lighting to better enable her to see around the room during the nighttime, especially when she used the commode. However, be mindful that the priority was to enable her to see the danger spots (commode access pathway). Soft pastels can relax, sooth and support, but stronger, more direct lighting is necessary in some locations. For instance, as her eyesight diminished, a stronger, more direct light was used.

Colors

Generally, certain colors can enhance specific moods; for instance, **earth tones** tend to relax people and are suited for conversation, recuperation, etc. These colors include beige, off-white and variations on the theme. Blue and gray are often used in corporate boardrooms and work areas because they tend to stimulate and energize. Red creates excitement and sometimes agitation, while pink reduces tension and is often used in prisons to reduce violence.

Example—"Bringing the Outdoors In"

As a nature-enthusiast and outdoorsman, I try to bring the outdoors into my home whenever possible, through artwork, live trees/plants and related efforts. In my bedroom, I have a small, tabletop artificial ponderosa pine behind which I have a string of blue holiday lights on the floor, activated on a timer. At the prescribed time, the lights go on and the resulting silhouette of the tree with the background blue light reminds me of sunsets in the woods. To further enhance the effect, the morning light casts a wonderful morning glow onto the tree and a realistic shadow is projected onto the bedroom wall…right near artwork of a woods scene (with trees and shadows). The effect created by lighting both at night and in the morning is surprising and quite supportive.

Wall Color

As a photographer, I am especially sensitive to my surroundings visually. In my bedroom, which overlooks a lake, I painted the walls with my own formula…mixing a subtle blending of traditional off-white paint with a hint of blue (rather than black, commonly used in off-white blends). After many attempts, I came up with a mix that captured the essence of looking into a crystal or iceberg. In the early morning or late afternoon when the light is right, the shadows in the room and behind the doors have just the right hint of blue to make it look like...you guessed it...you are gazing at a crystal or iceberg. Very cool!

Summary of lighting tips and essentials to remember[1]:

- Pathway lighting (and all other steps) should illuminate dark areas of potential accidents, avoiding shadows. Automation helps manage the lighting. White lines painted on steps also help prevent problems.
- Stairways (in or outside) can be lit using "rope-lights" attached to the underside of the railings.
- Fluorescent bulbs and tubes provide better lighting with reduced energy costs compared with traditional incandescent bulbs.
- Sheer curtains and woven lampshades allow more light into a living space, compared with heavy draperies across windows and sliding doors.
- Targeted, strong (possibly halogen) lighting should focus on "task locations"...for reading, hobbies, craft work, cooking, etc.
- Countertops in the kitchen should be well-defined with a contrasting edge, to prevent "missing" the counter.
- Dining areas need ambient, indirect lighting rather than direct task-lighting.
- Nighttime lighting for safety requires illuminated wall switches, soft lighting, night lights and incandescent fixtures on dimmers. Automated motion-activated lighting can be very useful, as I have learned in our home.

---

[1] Source: Lighting Your Way to Better Vision, The Center for Design for an Aging Society; www.centerofdesign.org Copyright 2006

- Lighting in closets is important for various reasons and fluorescent tubes can be very helpful. They don't use much energy and do not give off heat.
- Ambient light (indirect lighting) reduces glare. Consider torchiere lights or fluorescent fixtures out of sight.

Aromas

The power of smell is the strongest of our sensory abilities. Aromas remind us of our past, inspire and stimulate us…and can relax and soothe. Historically, cultures have utilized scents in various aspects of life, including infusing the sails of boats with aromas…even the bricks of buildings have had scents put into the mix!

In our house, we kept the bleach and other strong odors away from the living quarters. For disinfectant, we used natural aromas such as **lemon and lavender** in household products and cleansers. In Mom's commode, we used a splash of lavender cleaner to keep the room fresh and smelling nice. (Lavender has been used for generations to relax and soothe.)

Aromas can stimulate appetite. Try using vanilla or variations of it.

Sounds and Music

As a performing musician, I realize the benefits of appropriate, supportive sounds to enhance one's life. Our emotional state of mind, or wellness, can be enhanced by utilizing certain senses including sounds. In my office, I use either classical or jazz to manage my emotional state. Yes, I utilize music to energize or relax…depending upon the stress factors at the moment. For Mom (and Dad), relaxing music was used for insomnia and in hospital settings to encourage rest and sleep. White noise is referred to as sounds that have been proven to affect certain parts of the brain responsible for emotions. Frequently, white noise is not music but simply sounds, real and artificial. You can purchase sounds/music for therapeutic applications at your local retailer. I have found that certain instruments are conducive for rest and recuperation; they include harp, piano, guitar and stringed instruments of an orchestra. The effects of music depend not only on the instrument being played, but also on the music selections. The bottom line? Be creative, do some research and find sounds and music that work for your purposes. Note of caution: When using a CD carousel or MP3 player, be careful not to have the music too repetitive…it then becomes predictable and ineffective. (Try using the "shuffle" option.)

Creative Cuisine—Tastes Make Sense (Chapter Three)

Mealtimes are often key activities for seniors, especially when they are away from their own homes. The healthcare industry has been reevaluating the manner in which meals are served to residents and patients…in order to preserve personal dignity and grace for this critical part of the day. When Mom was in a facility recuperating from hip surgery, I hired an Aide to facilitate her eating and enjoyment of this special activity…mealtime. I was there, too, whenever possible.

While we have addressed this topic in Chapter Three, suffice it to say that creativity will make mealtimes more enjoyable for everyone. Some suggestions include:

- Adding ice cream to liquid nutritional supplements
- Enhance subtle flavors with flavor extracts (vanilla, fruit flavors, etc.) For instance, add vanilla extract to enrich vanilla milkshakes…as needed.
- Mix flavors…for variety. Mom loved the combination of mint with chocolate; hence, in her brownies she always added a dash of mint to the mix for a refreshing spin on the traditional brownie. (Speaking of brownies, be very careful of using berries, nuts and seeds when cooking for seniors…they can cause real problems…especially when diverticulitis is a possibility. When in doubt…leave it out!)
- Use no-salt/no msg additives for added flavor, Mrs. Dash or a similar product.
- Be vigilant! I once found one of our Aides serving Mom (with limited eyesight) a sandwich…WITH TOOTHPICKS IN THE SANDWICH! Another time, Aides were serving Mom soup…WITH BONES IN THE SOUP! You should always discuss mealtimes and important criteria/priorities with those who serve and support your loved ones…. before accidents happen!

Visual Stimulation

Mom's declining eyesight made it challenging to create an environment that soothed and supported her...visually.

We first identified the colors that she could enjoy and proceeded to plant flowers of such colors. In my earlier book, I mentioned the concept of "***Celebrations of Color***" throughout the home. By that I mean, out of each window in the home, there should be a splash of color...whether in a plant, flower, or garden railroad. There is something stimulating and colorful from every vantage point. During the holidays, I decorated the home with the same passion and commitment, using strategic placement of mirrors and holiday lighting. To be specific, the dining room had a tabletop tree with lights.

The room also had a large mirror, which further enhanced the lighting by multiplying it. Through the glass windows of the dining room, there could be seen an orange tree (complete with dwarf fruit) fully lighted for the holidays with tiny blue lights. So, when Mom was wheeled through this room, she enjoyed both the patio orange tree, but also the dining room lights.... all multiplied by the mirror! A small investment in lights can create a *visual winter wonderland!*

Our outdoor garden railroad ran around the goldfish pond and brick patio. It provided a relaxing and peaceful setting for meals and conversation. (But due to its backyard location, Mom later preferred the front of the house so she could be accessible to neighbors passing by. As for the garden railroad, her favorite car was the yellow coach...which could be seen from her bedroom window.

Dad's Memorial Garden— (see also Chapter Nine)

I created a Memorial Garden to my Dad in our backyard complete with sailboat statue. This garden was visible from various vantage points around the house and included colors of plants chosen by Mom for her enjoyment.

Tactile...Touch

The ability to touch and feel is critical, especially for totally blind individuals. Since Mom had limited visibility, this was not a priority of ours, but one of our Aides designed and made a doll for Mom to hold and appreciate. Like many girls, Mom enjoyed playing with dolls and later in life collected those with ceramic heads. It was especially kind of our Aide to build the doll and all the clothes...with Mom's creative input. (This project became a nice activity for both of them.)

In communities and healthcare facilities, tactile and other sensory elements are used to differentiate floors, hallways and other locales in the residence...helpful to both cognitive and visually impaired individuals. Colors, shadow boxes, flooring and lighting can be factors to consider.

CHAPTER SEVEN

"The Game Changer— Mom's Broken Hip

OK, things are going along fine. Your loved ones are somewhat healthy and content at home with limited support as needed...and then....life changes instantly!

You get the call from Florida that your Mom broke her hip and will be coming home to live with you and your family after rehab. <u>Now what?</u>

Before you visit the local do-it-yourself retailer...or perhaps call homecare agencies, let's do some basic research and preparation for what you're getting into. Take a deep breath, and tell yourself, you <u>can</u> do this!

Unfortunately, most families wait until there is a major medical mishap, accident or life change before they do anything to prepare for aging and the support of loved ones. The most frequent *life change* is a broken hip. In and of itself, a broken hip is fairly common and so is the surgery; however, it is helpful to get an understanding of the implications it causes for your family.

Here's Our Story

Mom crossed her leg on the side of her bed, and *the leg snapped!* Ouch! The mere thought of it turns my stomach. Dad was alive then and promptly called for help. (We had a homecare Aide with the folks to provide constant care at this time.) They activated the **"First Alert"** button. (Perhaps you've seen them advertised on television. These essential communication devices summon external emergency personnel to your home via a single transmitter in your house.) Although I was not present at the time of the incident, I was told within a few minutes that there were emergency respondents in the room tending to Mom.

A Woman of Grace & Dignity

Although in pain and embarrassment, a woman of grace and dignity prevailed. Picture this: a woman writhing in pain and surrounded by unfamiliar attendants. While being transferred to the gurney, she asked—"How do I look?" She continued, "I need some color." When translated this meant she needed some lipstick; a prerequisite to any social and public appearance in her generation. I tell this story at every presentation because it reflects the dignity and style of a generation long since passed. Looking good when you left the house was a way of living. Mom always said, "Look the part...be the part! The way we look contributes to the way we are treated." How true! (She was not a prima donna or princess, just a child of a different generation with different norms and standards than today. It was a period of dignity, grace and style.

The subsequent hip surgery was an experience for us all. I learned that although Mom was not an alcoholic, she had to experience "detox" due to her daily aperitif. I was told that our bodies become accustomed to such indulgences and must be purged before surgery, sometimes requiring a couple of days. (As if the broken hip wasn't disruptive enough!)

Sundowning

After the surgery came rehabilitation, which was done at a local facility that was attached to a continuing care community. In my daily visits, I eventually was subjected to what I later referred to as "***The Demon of Darkness***"; also frequently referred to as **"Sundowning"**. My introduction to this condition came as I was leaving early in the evening, after supper. I learned that without warning, many patients on Mom's wing became agitated…wanting to walk around, get out of bed, take off clothing, become loud and irritating, etc. I noticed that she too was experiencing some of these disturbing symptoms. As I probed for an explanation of this unusual behavior, I was told that sundowning usually occurs as a result of several factors, including the aftermath of a life change or injury, surgery, blood loss, unfamiliar surroundings and medication. The remedy is frequently a shot of some strong medication, (which sometimes has serious side affects), but I understand there now is a wafer or pill that is absorbed directly into the patient quickly without a shot.

I was not one to sit idle as my Mom suffered, so I promptly developed a process of options for Mom's care when she was sundowning. (see below)

When the "Demon of Darkness" knocked on my Mom's door, the nurses and Aides had some options and considerations...before administering medication.

Aids, Nurses and other Caregivers for Marie Oakes

On behalf of our family, I send our deepest thanks and appreciation for your kindness, patience and compassion in supporting Marie through these difficult times. We know you have many patients, but there is only one Marie in our family and she is a sweet and kind lady who needs your help. She certainly can use all the help and support she can get right now and we are counting on YOU! Please treat her as you would your own Mom.

Background:

Tell the supporting Aide of your Mom's interests, background, etc. The better informed they are, the better the staff can relate and interact with your Mom.

Habits and Related Items of Interest:

She enjoys background music
She cannot read magazines or newspapers well any longer.
She loved to garden and enjoys the outdoors in the backyard.

Eating:

She used to eat anything
Enjoys lobster salad rolls from Stop and Shop
She is color-conscious and creative

It is common knowledge that we are all sensory beings who are affected by our surroundings through our senses. Although the following tactics may not always have been effective when the ***"Demon of Darkness"*** (Sundowners Syndrome) visited Marie, they are worth consideration.

1. **Television-** perhaps some TV might distract her. The Travel, History or HGTV channels sometimes work for her. The television has a timer that can be programmed for automatic shut-off. She has **Macular Degeneration** and, therefore, may not see the television very well; be aware of this.
2. **Agitation**—if she wants to get out of bed, let her. Walk with her around the house (or floor, if in a hospital). Why not?
3. **Video-** the television has a VCR in it for Marie's convenience. The videos in her room are for her use and feel free to use them. One is of a family visit to Bermuda.... the other is a show from the Travel Channel.
4. **Tactile**—sometimes a stuffed animal or doll can provide tactile comfort. Pet therapy can also help...using live pets.
5. **Food/beverages**—sometimes warm milk can help induce sleep. Find out your Mom's favorite drink and consider

giving her a "nightcap"....it is advisable to consult with a doctor or nurse about any use of alcohol.

6. **Aromatherapy**
   - A tiny tube of trial size "Peace of Mind" cream is in her room near the window. It is to be applied on ear-lobes and temples to calm and provide some solace. Offer it to her.
   - **Lavender pillow spray** is near her phone on the table. It can be used before bedtime *sparingly* around her pillow.
7. **Music-** Mom likes music and is accustomed to it at home. Although she normally does NOT like machines or music going at night, the CD player near the window can be left ON 24/7 at a very low setting. The low volume should provide a settling, soft reassuring support for her.

Mom returned home as soon as feasible, where she continued to receive excellent care and support from family, friends and our capable team of professionals. She passed in 2009...at home, as she preferred, never alone, (as I promised our Father)

CHAPTER EIGHT

Painful Lessons Learned

Lesson One: *Aging*-in-Place... *Dying* at Home

The first lesson occurred when Mom died at home. It is a true and unfortunate ordeal that my family endured at one of the most precious and critical times of life...and death. As a result of this experience, I co-authored a proposed bill for the CT State Legislature.

As promised to my Dad, Mom was never alone. We were fortunate to secure Certified Nursing Assistants 24/7 for Mom's homecare. When Mom died at home (with Aide present), the First Alert button was pushed (summoning emergency personnel, which included the local Police Services). Within moments, Mom's bedroom was filled with our team, medical personnel, clergy, and the police. When I arrived, I was told that we all had to **vacate the premises** and **provide a key to the Police Officer**! I explained my role, to no avail. I proceeded to spend the next 90 minutes in the living room on the phone with our attorney, who had never heard of such abuse! He explained that I would be arrested, if I did NOT comply! (To leave our family home under orders of the police!) Meanwhile, Mom was taken away to the funeral home after the doctor attended to her. My immediate reaction was to have them arrest me...in front of television cameras! The visual impact of a son being carried out of the family home when his Mother died, and being aired on the evening news, would have been effective, I thought. But cooler and calmer minds prevailed...I left and subsequently wrote an Op-Ed piece for the local newspaper. (*West Hartford...a Great Place to Live, Lousy Place to Die!*)

The following Monday (the incident was on a Friday), we were advised that the *town ordinance* required the Police to secure the premises after the death of the (permanent and full-time) resident(s). The rationale was to prevent fraudulent access to the home by unauthorized visitors and family members who could take advantage of an unsecured property/home and steal things. While this reasoning has merit, there must be a better, more civilized and sensitive way. Eight months later, I co-wrote a draft proposal to the CT State Legislature. Although the bill was rejected due to cost concerns, the effort has not ended and future efforts will, hopefully, improve procedures and policies to preserve the dignity and respect for grieving family members at the time of death, while protecting the estate and its contents.

Until a solution is adopted, I recommend the following:

- Make a **list of authorized personnel** who should have access to the home at and *after* the death of its sole resident. Had such a listing been available at our home, we would not have had to vacate it. As we have mentioned earlier, **this listing could be included with the medication summary,** often contained in a vial in the refrigerator.

- In Connecticut, <u>each town</u> has its own interpretation of this ordinance. I suggest you research how your local Probate Court handles death-at-home (of sole resident).

Lesson Two—A Stranger in Your Home

As you know by now, it is critical to protect your family, finances and well-being during the caregiving process. The benefit of finding help through an agency is that they assume all financial and legal responsibilities in terms of protecting your family against theft, damage...and the agency takes care of the tax/payroll ordeal. But, of course, there is no free "lunch". There is a price to pay for convenience. Our family elected to assume all responsibility for contracting homecare.

You can do all you can to check backgrounds of applicants and call references, etc. But sometimes it's simply not good enough. One of our Aides accused my family of treating her "differently" because she was from Kenya. (As a human resource professional, I am well aware of the definitions and critical nature of discrimination cases.) Not only did I NOT know of her country of origin, but it did NOT influence her qualifications for the job she was performing. This tidbit of information was irrelevant to her job. Nonetheless, she demanded $5,000 payment or else she was going to make our lives miserable! Well my friends, this is called **"extortion"** After eight months of fighting this matter at the state level, it was apparent to my family that we were presumed guilty until proven innocent. We were advised to pay her off (because our defense would have cost much more than $5,000). **We were told that the system was "broken" and we should settle with her out of court!** This is very upsetting to every law-abiding citizen who wishes to do the right and legal thing as they care for their aging loved ones. This is wrong and must be corrected, but until it is….**be aware of the "stranger in your home".**

Suggestions:

- Protect or remove valuables in your home
- Protect your personal passwords and social security number and other confidential information.
- Shred unnecessary tax and other forms that reveal personal information.
- Remove cash and jewelry from the premises.
- All caregiver applicants must complete job application that includes the phrase *"Be advised that the owners of these premises reserve the right to use surveillance devices and or services for the protection of the residents"*.

CHAPTER NINE

Legacy Matters

"Gone but not forgotten"

When my Mom was being interred in the church memorial garden, I asked the pastor for some of her ashes, to which he replied, "Sure." As he shared her remains with me, he asked if this (distribution) was uncomfortable to me. I said that it was not only *not uncomfortable*, but appropriate for me to be active in this part of her journey. Why should I abandon her at death?

Regardless of your religious affiliation, , and personal beliefs, the idea of preserving and maintaining memories and homage to your deceased loved ones can be an important part of the transition for you and your family.

Some options to consider: (whether in a park, church/temple, private residence or community)

- Plant something "living", such as a tree or bush
- A statue of something of relevance to your loved one (see story below) that will endure the test of time!
- Many churches and parks sell *bricks* with names inscribed on them.

- A dedicated water feature/garden in a park or public garden
- A bench
- A special *event* in tribute to your loved ones. (see story below)

"Memorial Garden at Home"

Our family has a nautical background. Growing up on Long Island, NY, we were accustomed to sailing and power boating. So when my Dad passed, I ordered a custom-made statue of a sailboat. This five-foot, 400 lb, ***statue*** was placed strategically in our backyard (insert). Mom considered it a memorial to Dad that she could see from various points around the house. Special care was taken so she could see it from her wheelchair! We planted a garden surrounding it with colors that Mom selected and could see. (Macular Degeneration limited her visual enjoyment…and caused a great deal of frustration, especially for such a creative, visual artist.) The colors of the flowers in this garden just happened to be the colors of Dad's alma mater …the University of Michigan! The family home was on a large pond and the placement of the statue was in such a position as to make it seem that it was <u>*actually on the water!*</u> When the house was sold after Mom's death, the sailboat statue was relocated to the same park where the family railroad operates.

"A Wish List"

During Mom's care at home, one of our Aides collected a "wish list," essentially a collection of various wishes Mom expressed. After Mom died, this Aide collected all her wishes…. placed them in an envelope…and attached it to a helium balloon. The note on the envelope read, *"Mrs. Oakes, all of your wishes have come true.*" A truly moving sentiment shared by an exceptional Aide.

Hooked Rug Exhibit

As a hooker (of rugs), my Mom was a founder of the Association of Traditional Hooking Artists, ATHA, and was a skilled instructor. In recognition for her skill, her legacy and the craft itself, her rugs are available for special exhibits and displays for all to enjoy and appreciate. Although she was a renowned authority on traditional rug hooking, to my knowledge, no one had ever exhibited her rugs during her lifetime. I am especially pleased that I have been able to secure two exhibits so far for her rugs since her passing.

Garden Railroad in Local Park

In an earlier chapter, you recall we had a miniature railroad in our backyard. It was located in a nice, relaxing sanctuary. The railroad was designed with discretion in mind. At a distance of ten feet, you couldn't see the tracks or the railroad with the exception of an occasional rooftop of a model building. Mom and Dad both commented how **it would be so nice to** *share the railroad with others.* So, after Mom died in 2009, I contacted a local park, which was coincidentally building a *Sensory Garden* at the time, and I convinced them that a miniature, garden railroad in their new garden would enhance their mission and add a new dimension. They agreed to build it if I would design it. So with the help of park personnel, family members and friends, the Wickham Park Railroad (visit YouTube under "Wickham Park Railroad") was constructed and celebrated its first operating season in 2010.

Without a budget, the railroad relied on my family's engines and cars, including Mom's favorite yellow coach. Since she was suffering from Macular Degeneration and her vision was impaired, she could still appreciate the yellow car running in the garden foliage… the contrast worked for her and she could see it from her bedroom window. Now that she is gone, her car, and the other rolling stock, is now enjoyed by all ages and abilities in this new park railroad.

Some quotations on "Legacy Matters"

The following poem was left in Mom's bedroom the day she died. The funeral home left it for us. I must admit, it still elicits tears. Take a moment to enjoy and reflect—

REMEMBER ME—anonymous author
Remember me whenever—
You see a sunrise,
You see a star
You see a rainbow,
Or woods in autumn colors from afar

Remember me whenever—
You see the roses,
Or seagulls sailing high
…in the sky of blue

Remember me whenever—
You see waves,
Shining in the sun.
And remember,
I'll be remembering you!

Remember me whenever—
You see a teardrop,
Or meadows still wet with
The morning dew.

Remember me when—
You feel love
Growing in your heart.
And remember,
I'll be remembering you.

-Unknown author

Your Home, Your Castle

When I give a presentation on aging or caregiving, I often end with a song or two, played on acoustic guitar. The following lyrics are from my favorite tune, written by David Roth. I have recorded it on YouTube so you might want to check it out. (The Chuck Oakes Channel, YouTube)

LEGACY—David Roth, composer and performer
An aging man, a younger one
And a woman in her prime
Connected by their circumstance of birth.
A Father, son and daughter all obsessed to find
The mark that each will leave upon this earth.

Verse:
Alone in his apartment, in his favorite easy chair
The aging man endures his failing health
Now the days preoccupied, arranging his affairs
Netting up the value of his wealth.
He says a prayer and falls asleep and somewhere in a dream.
He's searching for his children and he's calling out to them.
Will I leave enough behind to help them get along?
Please tell me, how will I be counted when I'm gone?

Chorus:
It won't be by your worldly goods.
It won't be by your gains.
Not among possessions you bequeath.
But wisdom, grace and kindness
And the power of your love will be.
The measure of the legacy you leave.

Verse:
Working day is over for the woman in her prime
Alone now in her office she looks around.
An unfulfilling business is the only sight she sees.
The ticking of the clock, her only sound.
She closes up and locks the door and trudges down the hall.
Take a window seat that evening on the train.
She stares out at the darkness, but the only thing she sees…
A reflection of her weariness and strain.
Her mind begins to wander, she remembers all the years.
Of the struggles and persistence that goes into such careers.
Here she was with everything she worked so hard to win…
And such an empty feeling burning deep within.

Here's to every aging person, and to all those in their prime.
And to passing on the love that they receive.
For wisdom, grace and kindness,
And the power of their love will be…
The measure of the legacy they leave.
The power of their love will be,
The measure of the legacy they leave.

CHAPTER TEN

Helpful Information and Resources

As a caregiver, you will need help! Whether directly or indirectly...volunteer or paid, you will ultimately need to reach out for information and assistance at some point. Knowing when and where to go for help is critical to your sanity and effectiveness as a caregiver. In my experience, my family and I connected with the following experts for information, guidance and "best practices":

- Elderlaw attorney
- Financial advisor
- CPA/tax professional
- CT Commission on Aging (advocates for the elderly and families)
- Area Agencies on Aging (non-governmental source of advocacy; CT has several offices which serve districts)
- CT Department of Labor (a great source for homecare employment matters)
- Homecare agencies (an option we used for awhile until we assumed all responsibilities ourselves)

- Referral services, such as "A Place For Mom" (which serve as brokers for residential communities and resources. They get compensated by the communities they serve.

Organizations, Associations and Other Resources

Children of Aging Parents, CAPS
www.caps4caregivers.org
A non-profit organization whose mission is to assist the nation's nearly 54 million caregivers of the elderly or chronically ill with reliable information, referrals and support. CAPS is a member of Independent Charities of America. 1609 Woodbourne Road, Suite 302A, Levittown, PA 19057 800-227-7294

AARP
1-888-OURAARP (687-2277) Mon-Fri 8-8 ET
601 E. Street NW, Washington, DC 20049 www.aarp.org

National Resource and Policy Center on Housing and Long Term Care
www.aoa.dhhs.gov/Housing/modifications.html.

CareGuide   1-888-389-8839
www.careguide.com An award-winning site of resources, referral network, care providers, services, articles, interviews and other helpful information. They provide management of care for loved ones usually through an

employer's Employee Assistance Program (EAP); however, they do provide "retail" services...for a fee.

Medicare

1-800-633-4227 Available 24 hours a day; TTY users should call 1-877-486-2048 www.medicare.gov

Administration on Aging—Elders & Families www.aoa.gov/eldfam.asp
Alzheimer's Association: www.alz.org
American Association of Homes and Services for the Aging: www.aahsa.org
Caregivers & Companions: www.caregivershome.com
Centers for Medicare and Medicaid Services: www.medicare.gov
ElderCare Location: www.eldercare.gov
Family Caregiver Alliance: www.caregiver.org
National Alliance for Caregiving: www.caregiving.org (presents reviews of web sites, videos, newsletters and more.)
National Council on the Aging: www.ncoa.org
National Family Caregivers Association: www.nfcacares.org
NOCA Benefits Checkup: www.benefitscheckup.org
Taking Care of Yourself as a Caregiver: www.careguide.com
Today's Caregiver: www.caregiver.com (discussion forum and links)
U.S. Administration on Aging: www.aoc.gov

Retail Sources: **catalogs of helpful devices and gadgets**

HSN Catalog Service, Inc.
Patrickf@hsn.net 216-831-6191 X 230

MaxiAids catalog
Products for independent living 800-522-6294

Independent Living Aids, Inc.
Can-Do Products for your active, independent life
1-800-537-2118 www.independentliving.com

Improvements 1-800-642-2112 www.safetyzone.com

Living Air
Electronic air purification systems, 612-780-9388
9199 Central Avenue NE Blaine, MN 55434

Leyden Aromas
A great source for small to large air enhancement systems and nebulizers.
800-754-0668

The New England Assistive Technology Marketplace (NEAT)
An information and resources service to individuals interested in various types of *assistive technology*. A fabulous resource.
1-866-525-4492, 860-243-2869 Info@neatmarketplace.org

Vision Dynamics
A Connecticut retailer specializing in visual aids.
203-271-1944 www.visiondynamics.com

Books and Periodicals

Caring for Your Aging Parents
A complete guide for children of the elderly by Robert R. Cadmus, M.D. Prentice-Hall, Inc., Englewood Cliffs, New Jersey, 1984

The Complete Guide to Eldercare
A.J. Lee and Melanie Callender, Ph.D.
Barron's Educational Series, Barron's, New York, 1998

Aging Parents and You
A complete handbook to help you help your elders maintain a healthy, productive and independent life by Eugenia Anderson-Ellis.
Marsha Dryan Master Media, New York, 1988

How to Care for Aging Parents by Virginia Morris, Workman Publishing, New York, 1996.

Home Safety Guide for Older People:
Check It Out/Fix it Up by Jon Pynoos and Evelyn Cohen, Serif Press, Inc. 1331 H. Street NW, Washington DC 20005 202-737-4650

Safety for Older Consumers, U.S. Consumer Product Safety Commission, Washington D.C. 20207 1-800-638-2772 free handbook

Other books on this topic:

- **How to Care for Aging Parents** by Virginia Morris and Robert Butler
- **The Complete Eldercare Planner: Where to Start, Questions to Ask and How to Find Help** by Joy Loverde
- **Coping With Your Difficult Older Parent: A Guide to Stressed-Out Children** by Grace Lebow, et al
- **Caring for Yourself While Caring for Your Aging Parents: How to Help, How to Survive** by Claire Berman

Additional contacts involving security and identify protection:
American Institute of Philanthropy
4579 Laclede Avenue, Suite 136
St. Louis, MO 63108-2103
314-454-3040

National Charities Information Bureau
19 Union Square West, 6th floor
New York, New York 10003-3395
212-929-6300

Philanthropic Advisory Service Council of the
Better Business Bureaus
4200 Wilson Boulevard, Suite 800
Arlington, VA 22203-1838
703-276-0100

Direct Marketing Association
Telephone Preference Service
P.O. Box 9014
Farmingdale, NY 11735-9014

Federal Trade Commission
Boston Regional Office
101 Merrimac Street, Suite 810
Boston, MA 02114-4719
617-424-5960

Chief Postal Inspector –Postal Crime Hotline
475 L'Enfant Plaza, SW, Room 3100
Washington, DC 20360
202-268-4298 or -4299

FBI's Internet Fraud Complaint Center: www.ifccfbi.gov
Identity Theft Resource Center: www.idtheftcenter.org
Privacy Rights Clearinghouse: www.privacyrights.org
Free handbook from the Federal Trade Commission:
"ID Theft: When Bad Things Happen to Your Good Name"
www.ftc.gov/bcp/coline/pubs/credit/idtheft.htm
or call AARP at 888-687-2277

If you suspect identity theft, contact the credit reporting agencies and place a "fraud alert" on your accounts.

- Equifax: 888-766-0008 or www.equifax.com
- Experian: 888-397-3742 or www.experian.com
- TransUnion: 800-680-7289 or www.transunion.com
- Federal Trade Commission: 877-438-4338

Parting Comments—

As a caregiver, it is critical that you maintain your health and spirit. Do all you can for those you support and serve, but don't forget YOU. Knowing when and where to reach out for help is important for YOUR survival. I have provided some resources for your consideration, but there are many others. Stay connected!

ABOUT THE AUTHOR

Chuck Oakes

O ften described as a *"Renaissance Man"*, Chuck's career began in Los Angeles at the age of eight, singing and playing guitar under the tutelage of **The Kingston Trio.** Three years later, he moved to CT where he has lived until recently. After getting a business degree, he played the hotel lounge circuit as entertainer. Modeling and television commercials soon followed. (Chuck was *"The Stetson Man"* for Coty Cosmetics and opened for his friends, *the Kingston Trio* for several concerts.)

After years in the entertainment field, Chuck redirected his focus to the human resources industry as a corporate trainer, executive coach and consultant. He became an **Advisor to the President's** *Council on Hiring Workers with Disabilities* and wrote a self-help book "**WHEN THE PINK SLIP COMES HOME**" for displaced workers.

"Aging Matters"

Learning from his caregiving experience with his parents, Chuck wrote his experiences in **"MAKING YOUR HOME SENIOR-FRIENDLY"** to help others address similar challenges. Recognized by **the United Nations** for his accomplishments, he is now a member of two NGO committees.

Chuck is an entertaining and engaging speaker. When appropriate, audiences might see his Martin and Stetson come out during a program…a light ending that *enhances the message.*

"Do what you can…with what you've got…while you've got it. Life can change in a heartbeat. Savor every moment!"

Testimonial

"*Chuck's compassionate and pragmatic reflections on caring for older adults reveal deep understanding and uncommon sensitivity, gleaned from his own experiences caring for aging parents. His sensible, real-world insights are invaluable for anyone – family, friends, and policy makers alike—who endeavor to enable older adults and caregivers to navigate their journey together with dignity and respect.*"

Julia Evans Starr, Executive Director
CT Commission on Aging

Made in the USA
Middletown, DE
07 April 2016